T5-AFD-241

A SKETCHBOOK OF EASY FLOWER DESIGNS

JUNE KAHL

DRAWINGS AND LETTERING

BY

ELLEN PARSONS

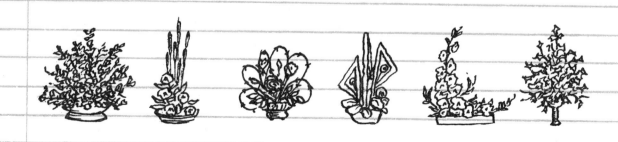

SPECIAL APPRECIATION
to
Mrs. Stuart Sunday
Mrs. Joseph Michels
Mrs. M. Nelson Bond
for cutting privileges in their gardens
and to
Miss Thelma Bauer, florist,
for her beautiful flowers

DEDICATION
In memory of Irma H. Crawmer
a good friend and dedicated teacher

A SKETCHBOOK OF EASY FLOWER DESIGNS

COPYRIGHT © 1981 BY JUNE R. KAHL   ISBN 0-941526-00-3

REPRINTED 1982, 1983, 1984

COVER BACKGROUND FROM A DOVER PUBLICATION • MARBELIZED

PAPERS • BY SAURMAN AND PIERCE

ALL RIGHTS RESERVED. THIS BOOK, OR PARTS THEREOF, MAY

NOT BE REPRODUCED IN ANY FORM WITHOUT PERMISSION OF

THE PUBLISHER.

PRINTED IN THE UNITED STATES

PROSPECT HILL

216 WENDOVER ROAD, BALTIMORE, MARYLAND 21218

CONTENTS

AUTHOR'S INTRODUCTION

Enjoy your flowers! To me this means being able to arrange your flowers, fruit, or foliage quickly and easily without having to spend hours agonizing over where to start, how long to cut the stems and which way to face the flowers.

This sketchbook with numbers is the result of years of experience in creating, showing, and teaching flower design. It is meant to be an easy to follow guide to enable the novice and not-so-novice to gain the confidence necessary to create attractive and interesting flower designs while learning the principles and elements of design and training the eye to see order in a flower arrangement.

Enjoy your flowers. Have fun with them. Expressing yourself through flower design can become more rewarding with each passing year.

BALTIMORE, MARYLAND

June R. Kahl

FLOWER ARRANGER'S WORKBASKET

A flower arranger is an artist working with live plant material and, like every artist, will need some basic tools and equipment. Keeping everything together in one place, ready to use, is the function of an arranger's workbasket. It should include:

1. FLOWER SCISSORS - with sharp straight blades to cut stems so they can absorb water easily

2. NEEDLEPOINT HOLDERS - 3", 1½", and one 3" pincup to hold flowers

3. FLORAL CLAY - to attach needlepoint holder to container

4. OASIS - floral foam to hold flowers in tall containers

5. CAN OPENER - to remove needlepoint holder from container

6. FLORAL WIRE - medium gauge (#20) to hold bent plant material in place

7. TALL CONTAINER - for water to condition flowers

5

FLOWER DESIGN BASICS

1. Size of container determines size of design as well as size and proportion of plant material.

2. Container shapes are:

RECTANGLE   ROUND   CYLINDER   COMPOTE

3. Containers with three legs are placed with one leg to the front.

4. The main line, stem #1, is the guide for the design. It is used to measure and place the remainder of the plant material.

5. Flowers have different forms. When making substitutions in a design, do not choose a different flower form.

    a. SPIKE  gladiolus, snapdragon, cattail
    b. ROUND marigold, aster, daisy
    c. OVAL ⚘ tulip, rose

6. Gradation of plant material is by size, form, color or texture.

    a. Lightest colors and smallest buds and flowers are placed to top and outer edges.

    b. Medium colors and medium flowers are placed in center of design.

    c. Largest and darkest flowers are placed at bottom of design.

7. Interest and variety are created by placing flowers at different heights and angles. Flowers should face in different directions, but they

should always look up.

8. Depth is created by placing some flowers behind others.

9. Leaves on branches should face front.

10. Branches and flowers are placed in the same direction in which they grew.

11. filler flowers and plant materials are used as transition between spike and round forms, filling in the spaces between them.

12. Some plant material should cover part of the edge of container.

13. The back of every design should be completed by using foliage to conceal bare stems and mechanics.

PREPARATION

1. flowers should be fresh and at the height of their perfection.

2. Condition all flowers immediately by cutting off at least one inch of stem, preferably under water. Strip off bottom leaves and place in deep tepid water. Leave in water several hours or overnight to harden before arranging. Exception — daffodils require shallow water.

3. Wash all foliage to remove dust. Remove broken or damaged leaves.

4. Start with a clean container and needlepoint holder.

5. Sit with container directly in front of you.

6. Attach needlepoint holder to dry container by rolling a piece of floral clay, between your two hands, into a long slender cigarette shape. Attach this to the outer edge of upside down needlepoint holder making sure you join the two edges together. Place needle-point holder in container. Press down hard at the same time giving it a slight twist. This will create a suction which holds the needlepoint holder in place.

7. Fill container with water before you start to make a design.

8. Remember that the first placement is the most important. Select the most beautiful and strongest plant material for #1. Cut #1 the correct height and place in proper po-sition because all that follow will be guided by it.

9. Determine height of first flower or branch by making it 1½ times the largest area of container plus the depth of the container.

10. Supplies may be purchased from florist or garden center.

DESIGN 1   ALL GREEN

PLACEMENT

ON NEEDLEPOINT HOLDER

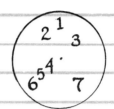

ATTACH

DESIGN 1

PHOTO

HERE

SUPPLIES

Container - small compote
     approx. 6" diameter
Needlepoint holder
     approx. 3" diameter
Plant material
     3 yucca
     3 Chinese evergreen
   1 spray variegated aucuba

PROCEDURE

#1, 2, 3 - yucca or sansevieria
     approx. 18", 16", 13"
#4, 5, 6 - Chinese evergreen or
   fatsia or large leaf begonia
#7 - aucuba or rhododendron
   spray ~ use smaller leaves
Some aucuba leaves should cover
   part of edge of container.

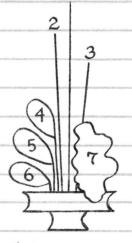

flower substitutions for #7
Spring: tulips   Summer: marigolds or zinnias
Fall: chrysanthemums

DESIGN 2   ASYMMETRICAL
a right triangle

ATTACH
DESIGN 2
PHOTO
HERE

PLACEMENT
on
NEEDLEPOINT
HOLDER

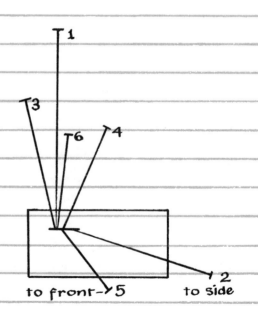

SUPPLIES

Container
   low rectangular
   approx. 12" long x
   8" wide x 2" deep
Needlepoint holder
   approx. 3" diameter
Plant material
   6 gladiolus
     (#1 through #6)
   8 filler green

PROCEDURE

#1 height is 1½ times the length of container
   plus depth. Place to left back.
#2 is ¾ height of #1. Place low over side front
   of container.
#3 is ¾ height of #2. Place slightly to left
   and forward of #1.
#4 is ¾ height of #3. Place slightly to right
   of #1, opposite #3.
#5 is ¾ height of #4. Place all the way for-
   ward on needlepoint with flowers
   facing upward and coming over the
   right front edge of container — at an
   angle slightly higher than #2.
#6 is slightly shorter than #3. Place exactly
   in center of needlepoint and lean
   slightly forward.
filler green plant material
   Cut all different lengths and place to
   accompany the 6 placements of the
   design.

VARIATIONS

Reverse the plant material — use foliage
for the line and flowers for the filler.

For a Christmas Design, use 6 straight
pieces of holly for #1, 2, 3, 4, 5, and 6. Use
5 red carnations for the filler.

11

DESIGN 3   VERTICAL

```
ATTACH
DESIGN 3
PHOTO
HERE
```

PLACEMENT
ON NEEDLEPOINT HOLDER

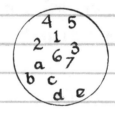

SUPPLIES

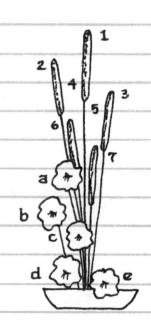

Container ~ small round
     approx. 6" diameter
Needlepoint holder
     approx. 3" diameter
Plant material *
     7 cattails - #1 through #7
     5 dahlias, approx. 2" dia.
filler green ~ dahlia foliage

*option
     Make use of your houseplants.
        5 sansevieria foliage - height of #1 - 20"
        3 chrysanthemums - medium size
        3 begonia leaves - large

PROCEDURE

Place #1 in center back of needlepoint, height 24"
   #2 to left of #1 and slightly forward
   #3 to right of #2 and slightly forward
   #4 to left back between #1 and #2
   #5 to right back between #1 and #3
   #6 to left front between #1 and #2
   #7 to right front between #1 and #3

Place dahlias on left side and across front of cattails with lowest flower coming partly over edge of container. Place foliage of dahlias gracefully around flowers.

NOTES

Always exaggerate the height of the plant material in a vertical design.

Each cattail is cut slightly shorter than the preceding one. This is called the "SHOE-LACING" method of placing plant material on the needlepoint.

DESIGN 4   LINE

ATTACH
DESIGN 4
PHOTO
HERE

PLACEMENT
ON NEEDLEPOINT HOLDER

1
2 .5
4   3

SUPPLIES

Container
   medium round
   approx. 10" diameter
Needlepoint holder
   approx. 3" diameter
Plant material
   3 bare or flower-
   ing branches
   2 tulips with foliage
Substitute dried branches such as manzanita,
winged euonymus, or dogwood for #1,2,3.
Substitute dried flowers such as artichokes
or protea for #4,5.

2   1

3

5
4

PROCEDURE

Place needlepoint holder off center in container.

#1 branch height is at least twice the diameter of the container. Place to left back of needlepoint.

#2 branch is 3/4 of #1. Place to left and front of #1.

#3 branch is 3/4 of #2. Place very low to right front.

#4 tulip - place in center of needlepoint and lean forward.

#5 tulip - place in back and to right of #4. Lean in same direction as #4.

Place tulip foliage so that it follows the same direction as flowers.

HOW TO BEND FRESH PLANT MATERIAL
for DESIGNS #5 and #8

1. Start halfway up stem.
2. Place both thumbs touching underneath stem with other fingers over top of stem.
3. Gently apply pressure.
4. Keep doing this as you move up to end of branch.
5. Repeat this procedure until the stem is bent as much as you want.

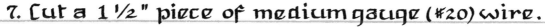
WIRE HERE

6. Bring tip around until it crosses main stem.
7. Cut a 1½" piece of medium gauge (#20) wire.
8. Bend around main stem and tip of plant material. Do it neatly and close together. Do not twist wire - just bend it around stem.

15

DESIGN 5   CIRCULAR
for dining room table

┌─────────────────────────────┐
│   │
│   │
│   ATTACH   │
│   DESIGN 5   │
│   PHOTO   │
│   HERE   │
│   │
│   │
└─────────────────────────────┘

PLACEMENT
on
NEEDLEPOINT
HOLDER

SUPPLIES

Container
    medium round
    approx. 12" diameter
Needlepoint holder
    approx. 3" diameter
Plant material
    8 forsythia branches
        36 inches long
    3 large roses
Filler plant material
    rose foliage

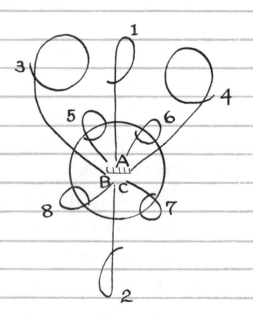

Substitute weeping willow—anthurium, peony, iris

16

DESIGN 1   PAGE 9

DESIGN 2   PAGE 10

DESIGN 4   PAGE 14

DESIGN 3   PAGE 12

DESIGN 5   PAGE 16

Carefully lift out center-
fold. Cut out one photo at
a time. Match with space
on designated page. Light-
ly moisten back of the
photo. Attach neatly in
place.

DESIGN 7   PAGE 20

DESIGN 6   PAGE 18

DESIGN 8   PAGE 22

DESIGN 9   PAGE 24

ESIGN 10   PAGE 26

DESIGN 11   PAGE 28

DESIGN 12   PAGE 29

PROCEDURE

PREPARATION OF BRANCHES

Strip all foliage and side branches from the forsythia. Cut off all the tips (3").

FOLLOW BENDING DIRECTIONS ON PAGE 15.

Bend and wire four 33" forsythia branches into large circles approx. 7" diameter.

Bend and wire four 28" forsythia branches into smaller circles approx. 5" diameter.

(If longer weeping willow branches are substituted, make multiple loops in the circles—a completely different look.)

Cut bottom of each branch stem with an X or crosscut—makes it easier to put on needlepoint.

TO ANGLE A BRANCH

Place branch upright on needlepoint and push branch down with thumb to desired angle.

#1, 2, 3, 4 – Place large circles at an angle to top and bottom, left and right on outer edges of needlepoint with circles facing towards center of container.

#5, 6, 7, 8 – Place smaller circles at an angle in between larger circles with circles facing outward over edge of container.

A, B, C – Place roses in a triangle pattern in center of needlepoint.

Place rose foliage lower than flowers in design and covering needlepoint.

DESIGN 6   LINE MASS

ATTACH
DESIGN 6
PHOTO
HERE

PLACEMENT
IN OASIS

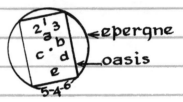

SUPPLIES

Container - candlestick with
   epergne adaptor
Oasis - cut to fill container
   extending 1½" above rim
Plant material*
   6 eucalyptus branches
   5 iris
filler plant material
   8 Baker fern
*spring option
   Any flowering fruit tree branches may be
used - apple, cherry, pear, plum, quince
flowers - tulips or daffodils

18

PROCEDURE

#1 height is twice height of candlestick. Place to center back.

#2 is ¾ height of #1. Place slightly forward to left of #1.

#3 is ¾ height of #2. Place slightly forward to right of #1.

#4 is ⅓ height of #1. Place opposite #1. Insert low at an angle upward in side of oasis.

#5 is ⅓ height of #2. Place opposite #2. Insert slightly higher than #4 at an angle upward in side of oasis.

#6 is ⅓ height of #3. Place opposite #3. Insert slightly higher than #5 at an angle upward in side of oasis.

Place bud flowers a and e to top and bottom in front of #1 and #4.

Place medium flowers b and d to right of a and e in front of #3 and #6.

Place largest flower c in center front between b and d.

Cut Baker fern in different heights. Place lower than flowers throughout design. Follow direction of iris. Cover the oasis.

NOTE

An epergne adaptor may be purchased from the florist.

DESIGN 7   MASS
          a symmetrical triangle
     FOR DINING ROOM TABLE

PLACEMENT
on
NEEDLEPOINT
HOLDER

ATTACH
DESIGN 7
PHOTO
HERE

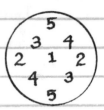

SUPPLIES
Container
    oval vegetable dish
    approx. 11" long x
    7" wide x 2" deep
Needlepoint holder
    approx. 3" or 4" di-
    ameter
Plant material
    9 snapdragons
        #1 height is 12"
    filler foliage
    10-12 Baker fern

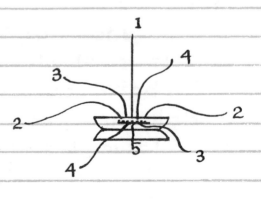

Use top of covered vegetable dish as a base.

20

Place needlepoint holder in center of container.

Place #1 in center of needlepoint holder.

Place the two #2's low and to each side. Part of flower should be over edge of container.

Place the two #3's slightly higher, in same direction as #2 - one to front and one to back.

Place the two #4's higher, in same manner as #3 - one to front and one to back.

Place the two #5's in front and back of #1 with part of flower over edge of container.

Place filler green under #1 and throughout design - in direction of and always shorter than the flowers.

LOOKING DOWN ON DESIGN

LOOKING AT SIDE OF DESIGN

Always work alternating from front to back. This makes the design the same on each side. Flowers are only slightly different in length. They appear to be different because of the angles at which they are placed.

DESIGN 8   ABSTRACT
                 for spring

```
┌─────────────────────────────┐
│                             │
│      ATTACH                 │
│      DESIGN 8               │
│      PHOTO                  │
│      HERE                   │
│                             │
│                             │
│                             │
│                             │
│                             │
│                             │
└─────────────────────────────┘
```

PLACEMENT
ON NEEDLEPOINT HOLDER

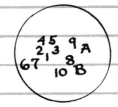

SUPPLIES
Container
   small round compote
   approx. 6" diameter
Needlepoint holder
   approx. 3" diameter
Plant material
   10 pussy willows
Filler flowers
   2 daffodils

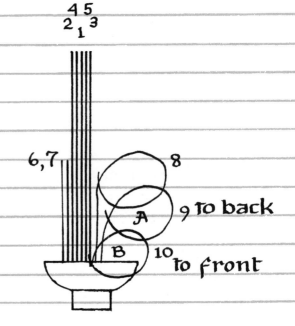

Bend and wire three pussy willows into circles. See page 15 for bending instructions.

Cut five straight pussy willows #1,2,3,4,5 the same length and as tall as possible with tops cut evenly. Place close together at left back of needlepoint.

Cut two pussy willows #6 and #7 shorter. Place against left side of #1.

Place tallest pussy willow circle #8 against right side of #1.

Place slightly larger circle #9 in back of #8, leaning slightly backward over edge of container.

Cut largest circle #10 short. Place in front of #1, slightly forward over edge of container.

Place filler flower A between #8 and #9. Cut so daffodil is in center of circle #9.

Place filler flower B between #8 and #10, slightly shorter than A and leaning slightly forward.

DESIGN 9   MASS

ATTACH
DESIGN 9
PHOTO
HERE

PLACEMENT

IN OASIS

```
     7    11      8
        9      10
            1
          4      5
     2              3
         6   12
```

SUPPLIES

Container · opaque goblet
    10 inches high
Oasis - cut to fill container and
    extend 1½ " above edge
Plant material
    12 holly branches
Filler flowers
    12 heather

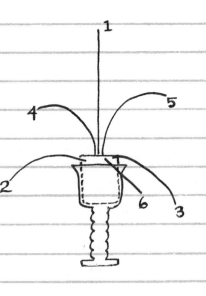

Oasis: buy a brick from florist. Use bread knife
to cut in shape of container. Remember to
extend 1½ " above edge. Soak in bowl of
water until completely saturated.

24

PROCEDURE

Use straight pieces of holly for main lines.
Cut off small side branches to make
single straight stems.

#1 length is 1½ times the height of the container.
Place in center of oasis.

All following plant material is cut shorter
than #1. Vary the lengths!
Place #2 low on left, in side of oasis.
    #3 lower and longer than #2, in right side.
    #4 higher on left.
    #5 higher than #4, on right.
    #6 forward center front, in side of oasis.

Place #7, 8, 9, 10, and 11 to back, using the same
placements as #2, 3, 4, 5, and 6.

Place #12 front forward, low and slightly to
the right of #6, in side of oasis, shorter than #3.

Filler flowers are placed at random throughout design. Cut different lengths and
place between holly but never taller.

ATTACH
DESIGN 10
PHOTO
HERE

PLACEMENT
IN OASIS

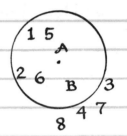

SUPPLIES

Container
   medium size pitcher
   approx. 10" height
Oasis
   cut to fill container and to
   extend 1½" above edge
Plant material
   4 small leaf holly branches
   4 larger leaf holly branches
   2 poinsettias
Filler plant material
   10 white pine branches

PROCEDURE

#1, 2, 3, 4 — small leaf holly
#5, 6, 7, 8 — larger leaf holly
A, B — poinsettias

#1 height is twice height of container. Place to rear left, deep in oasis.

#2 - shorter than #1. Place to left, slightly forward.

#3 - shorter than #2. Place front right. Insert at an angle upward in oasis.

#4 - shorter than #3. Place center front. Insert at an angle upward in oasis.

#5, #6 - follow direction of #1, #2-except shorter.

#7, #8 - follow direction of #3, #4-except shorter.

Place flower A toward back.
Place flower B diagonally to front.

Cut white pine various heights. Place the pine throughout design, following the direction of holly but never higher than holly. Make sure oasis is covered by the pine.

Give white pine a haircut!
Cut straight across the tips — about ½ ".
This makes the pine neater looking.

DESIGN 11   CRYSTAL

ATTACH
DESIGN 11
PHOTO
HERE

SUPPLIES
Container
   crystal cylinder
   approx. 9" height
Plant material
   2 stalks - Easter
   lily
Mechanics
   none

PROCEDURE

Strip off all foliage that will be under water.
Cut each stalk at an angle so that it can be
braced against the side of
container. This is what holds
the lilies in place.

Place #1 low against side and
bottom of container

Place #2 slightly higher a-
gainst opposite side of container.

28

Stems should always be placed
neatly and uniformly in any
crystal container regardless
of shape.

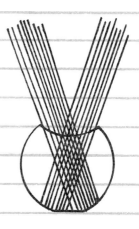

In a large round crystal container, crisscross the stems
in four directions.

In a tall crystal container,
place all the stems verti-
cally — filling the entire
container.

ATTACH

DESIGN 12

PHOTO

HERE

PLACEMENT

ON NEEDLEPOINT HOLDER

4 B
2 1 3
A 5 C

SUPPLIES

Container
   medium round
   approx. 10" diameter
Plant material
   5 mullein (tall roadside
   weed)
   3 geraniums with foliage

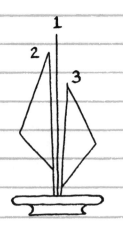

Yucca may be substituted for mullein. Do not
cut. Bend each piece <u>once</u> to form an angle.
Follow placement as for mullein.

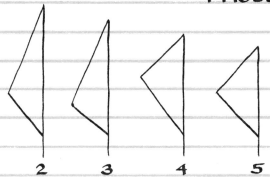

2   3   4   5

Make four different-
shaped triangles from
four stalks of mullein.

Cut a stalk of mullein into 3 pieces.

Cut two 1½" pieces of wire.
Insert wire into center of each
     cut end.
Bend to desired angle to form
     one triangle.
If wire slips, fill holes with
     Elmer's glue.

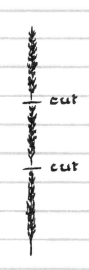

cut

cut

All triangles face outward toward edge of
     the container.

Place #1, straight piece of mullein, in the
          center of needlepoint holder.
     #2 to left of #1.
     #3 to right of #1.
     #4 in back of #1.
     #5 in front of #1.
Cut flowers A, B, C different heights and
     and place around #1.

31

GLOSSARY

ABSTRACT_ a creative art form in which plant material is used with space to create new images

CONDITIONING _ preparation of cut plant material before arranging

DESIGN ELEMENTS _ the basic, visual qualities of a design: space, line, form, size, color, texture, and pattern

FLOWER ARRANGING_ the art of organizing the design elements of plant material and other components according to design principles to obtain beauty, harmony, distinction, and expression

FILLER PLANT MATERIAL _ transitional plant material used to fill in between different plant forms

GRADATION_ a sequence in which there is regular and orderly change in size, form, color, or texture

GROOMING_ cleaning flowers to remove dirt and spray residue as well as dead or broken foliage or flowers

HARDENING _ to place plant material in water several hours before arranging

PRINCIPLES OF DESIGN_basic art standards used to organize design elements: balance, proportion, scale, rhythm, dominance, and contrast